MUSEUM PUZZLE-PICTURE BOOK OF
LIFE IN
ROMAN TIMES

Sponsored by the Museums Association

Heritage Books & Longman

A ROMAN FAMILY AT HOME

A rich Roman family prepares for a pleasant evening. Dinner is being cooked in the kitchen and a slave lights the lamps and candles. Father pays a merchant for a piece of furniture and the children play games.

Spot the differences

In this picture, eight things are missing or have been
changed in some way. See if you can spot them.
The answers are on the next two pages.

DID YOU FIND THESE THINGS?

The children's toy animal on wheels is missing. Roman children had plenty of toys. Girls had dolls' houses with furniture; boys had spinning tops, hoops and toys with wheels. They played on swings and seesaws; two of their favourite games were leap-frog and blind man's buff.

Part of the floor mosaic near the dog is missing. Mosaics were made by setting small pieces of naturally-coloured stone into a bed of cement to make patterns or pictures. A mosaic worker made the small pieces by placing a coloured stone across a sharp blade set in a block of wood and then tapping tiny segments from it with a hammer.

2

3

A gold brooch is missing from the mother's dress. Romans used pins and brooches to fasten their clothes. They also wore rings, necklaces and bracelets as ornaments. Some rich Romans had their jewellery buried with them when they died and these have sometimes been found by archaeologists.

The tall bottle standing in the kitchen has gone. These were big earthenware jugs called 'amphorae' and were used for storing liquids like wine and olive oil. The pointed end was used as a handle for pouring. The amphora held about 5 gallons (25 litres).

1

4

5

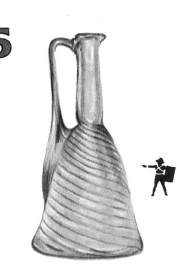

The glass jug is missing from the side-table. The Romans knew how to make beautiful things of glass and even though it is easily broken, some has survived. This is because they used to bury glass ornaments with people when they died and archaeologists have found many examples. Roman glass was too dark and thick to be made into clear windows. It could only be used in buildings to let in some light and give protection from bad weather.

The coins are missing from the merchant's hand. The Romans used money for buying and selling and for paying wages. Their coins were made of gold, silver, brass and bronze, according to value. The coins showed the Emperor's head on one side with his name. We know exactly when each Emperor reigned so that coins help to date a Roman site when they are found. There are many Roman coins to be seen in museums.

8

An oil lamp is missing from the small table. These little lamps were made of metal or pottery and were filled with olive oil. A wick fitted into the hole in the spout and the lamp was filled through the hole in the middle of the bowl. Romans also made candles by pouring tallow (melted animal fat) into an open container round a wick, then letting it set.

The hand-mirror held by the slave girl is missing. The Romans did not know how to make mirrors from glass so they used highly polished metal instead. It does not give a very good reflection so that Romans never saw themselves as clearly as we can.

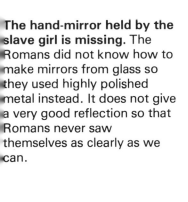

6

7

MARKET DAY IN A ROMAN TOWN

It is a busy shopping day in a Roman town. All kinds of things can be seen going on. The building on the left is an inn where men can be seen stacking wine barrels.

Some musicians play to entertain passers-by and a fine lady arrives in a litter carried by four slaves. A butcher is serving a customer with meat and the baker's shop next door is piled high with freshly baked bread. An army officer is telling an important citizen about some plans he has for the defence of the town. Some of his soldiers can be seen on the town walls behind.

The artist has made eight deliberate mistakes in the picture. See if you can spot them. The answers are on the next two pages.

Spot the deliberate mistakes

DID YOU SPOT THESE THINGS?

The musician outside the inn is playing a modern electric guitar. That is an instrument the Romans certainly did not have! They had many different kinds of stringed and wind instruments which were used in orchestras. They also enjoyed singing and children were taught to sing at school. No written records of Roman music have been found.

1

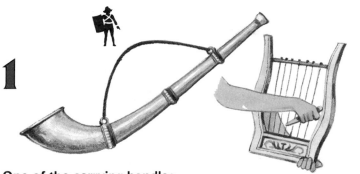

One of the carrying-handles is missing from the litter in which the lady is being carried by her four slaves. On long journeys she would have travelled in a two-wheeled cart drawn by horses; a litter like this one would have been much more comfortable for shopping and other short journeys.

2

3

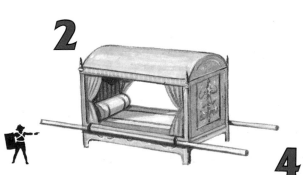

The man in the foreground is carrying milk bottles in a modern milk-delivery crate. He would have carried it in a jug. The Romans made pottery jugs and jars of all kinds and some were very beautiful – just as good as modern ones. Many have survived and can be seen in museums.

The name of the inn is the 'Ship' but the inn sign shows a modern steamship! The Romans used signs like these, either painted or carved from stone, to tell people what trades shops were carrying on. Some shop signs can be seen in the picture. There is one for the butcher's shop and another for the baker.

4

5

The scales on the butcher's counter are modern ones. He would really have used the kind shown here. It was called a 'steelyard' and was a metal beam balanced unevenly. The thing to be weighed was placed in the tray which hung from the short end of the beam and a weight was moved along the beam until it balanced. The weight was then read off against a scale marked on the beam.

7

The chopper the butcher is using has no blade. The Romans liked meat and at important feasts they would serve roast boar, venison, veal, mutton or beef. The butcher would also sell sausages and lard for cooking. When he had cut up his meat for the day he hung it up on hooks in his shop for customers to see, just as many modern butchers do.

8

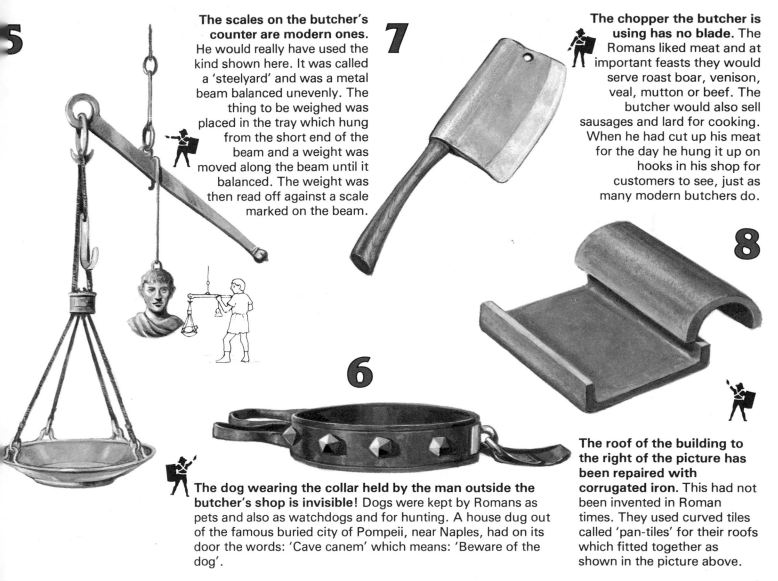

6

The dog wearing the collar held by the man outside the butcher's shop is invisible! Dogs were kept by Romans as pets and also as watchdogs and for hunting. A house dug out of the famous buried city of Pompeii, near Naples, had on its door the words: 'Cave canem' which means: 'Beware of the dog'.

The roof of the building to the right of the picture has been repaired with corrugated iron. This had not been invented in Roman times. They used curved tiles called 'pan-tiles' for their roofs which fitted together as shown in the picture above.

Jigsaw puzzle

These eight jigsaw pieces fit somewhere into the picture. Each one contains part of something used by the men in the picture, for their work. See if you can spot where the pieces fit and say what the eight things were for. The answers are given on the next two pages.

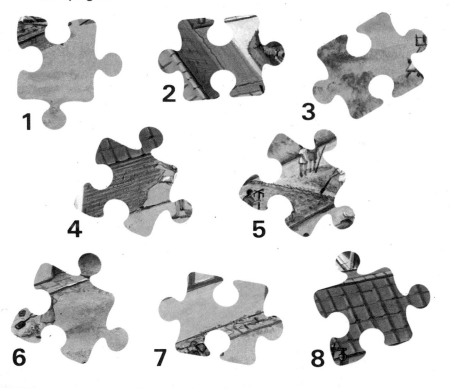

ROADSIDE INN

This picture shows a Roman inn being built beside a new road. The workmen have nearly finished it and some guests have just arrived in a two-wheeled cart.

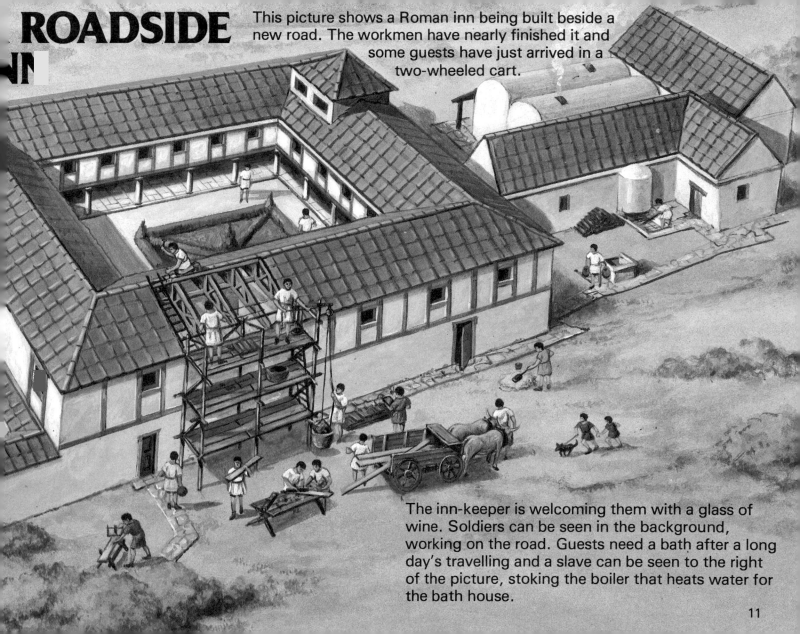

The inn-keeper is welcoming them with a glass of wine. Soldiers can be seen in the background, working on the road. Guests need a bath after a long day's travelling and a slave can be seen to the right of the picture, stoking the boiler that heats water for the bath house.

DID YOU FIND THESE THINGS?

This shows the wood plane on the bench in front of the scaffolding. Wood planes are used for giving timber a smooth finish. The workmen in the picture are carpenters and the tools they are using are very like modern ones. Examples of Roman tools can be seen in museums.

1

This shows the trowel being used by the plasterer working on the wall round the forecourt of the inn. Trowels like this have been found on many Roman sites and they are exactly like modern ones. The Romans liked to decorate the walls of rooms with painted pictures and for this they needed to have very smooth surfaces. Their plasterers were very highly skilled.

4

This shows the chisel the workman on the roof of the inn is using. Chisels are tools which have one end bevelled to give a cutting edge. They have a wooden handle and a wooden mallet is used with them. Wood carving is done with chisels and they are also used by sculptors to shape stone.

2

3

This shows the wood saw being used by the man cutting timber for the roof. Saws like this are still in use. They are called 'bow' saws and nowadays, instead of the frames being made of wood, they are of steel. Because they had such good tools, the Romans were excellent builders. In Rome they built blocks of flats several stories high.

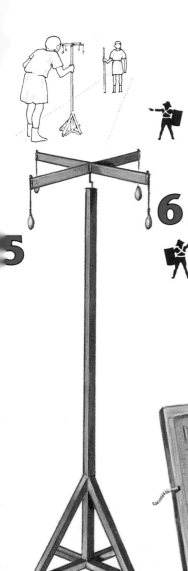

This shows the sighting instrument the surveyor is using. It was called a 'groma'. The groma was first lined up by means of the sighting bars, to be exactly at right-angles to the line of the road. By looking along the other sighting bar to a distant mark, the surveyor could then make sure the road was being built straight.

5

6

This shows the rope and pulley block fixed to the top of the scaffolding. Pulley blocks are used with ropes to give greater lifting power. They make it possible for the lift to be 'geared down' so that a long, easy pull will lift a heavy weight a small amount at a time. Ropes with pulleys are still used – for hauling up the sails of big sailing ships, for example.

8

This shows the spade being used by the workman behind the two children with the dog. He is mixing cement. Roman spades were made of wood with the blade encased in metal to give them strength. They were used by the Romans for many purposes. The army used them for digging trenches and for making roads; they were used on farms, and builders used them, as in this picture, for mixing concrete and cement.

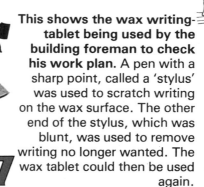

This shows the wax writing-tablet being used by the building foreman to check his work plan. A pen with a sharp point, called a 'stylus' was used to scratch writing on the wax surface. The other end of the stylus, which was blunt, was used to remove writing no longer wanted. The wax tablet could then be used again.

7

ROMAN HOLIDAYS

This book has shown, in pictures, how ordinary people lived in Roman times. The wealthy people who had country villas and slaves; the farmers who worked their land; the traders who kept shops and the workmen who built roads and inns for travellers. Much of it was very like life today; but this was only part of the story.

In the great city of Rome itself, where the Roman Emperor lived, life was very different. Wealth poured into Rome from all over the world. There were great warehouses in the business part of the city, filled with everything imaginable – wines, oil, dates, meats of all kinds, gold, silver, amber, ivory, incense, silks, spices, precious stones. They came from all over the world because Rome was the centre of a great Empire. There were plenty of slaves, taken in battle, to do all the dirty jobs and all the fetching and carrying, and the Romans had time on their hands. The city was also very crowded – with more than a million inhabitants – for people from all the surrounding lands were attracted to the greatest city in the world.

The Roman Emperors found themselves living in their palaces with swarming masses crowding the streets all round. If such numbers of people, many of whom were unemployed, were not to become rebellious, the Emperors had to find a way of keeping them contented. They did this by declaring public holidays and giving them free food and entertainment. At the time of the Emperor Claudius, not long after the death of Christ, there were as many as 200 public holidays declared in one year – that is at least one holiday for every working day!

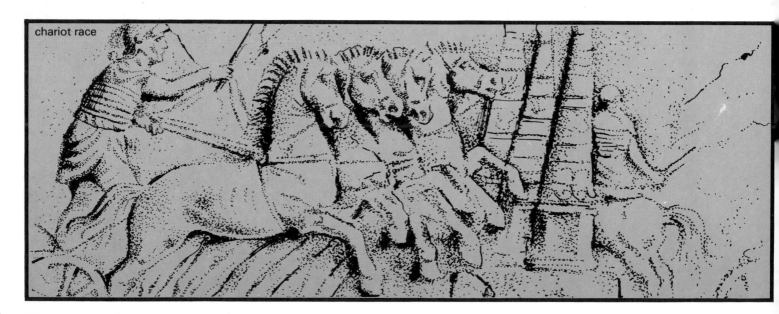

chariot race

CHARIOT RACES

Chariot races were one of the most popular of the Emperors' entertainments and they were staged in vast arenas, some of which could seat more than 250,000 spectators. The race track, called the 'Circus' or 'Amphitheatre', was a long rectangle between 440 – 660 yds long (400 and 600 metres) and about 220 yds wide (200 metres), rounded off at one end into a semi-circle. Two, three, and most often, four racehorses were harnessed to tiny, two-wheeled chariots and each race consisted of seven laps of the course. Four chariots took part in each race, the horses and drivers being given colours – Red, Blue, Green and White. It must have been a splendid sight as the four chariots lined up for the start. The horses decorated with pearls in their manes, their harnesses studded with silver plaques and the ribbons of their colours.

The chariot-driver stood upright in his chariot, helmet on his head, whip in hand, leggings fitted to his calves and thighs, dressed in his racing colours. The reins were bound round his body and he wore a dagger to cut himself free if there was an accident. Then they were off! The crowd roared as the four chariots made for the first corner. If a chariot turned too tightly it risked running into the corner post; if it ran too wide it might be hit by the chariot behind. Fourteen times they had to round those corners, all four teams trying to beat the others in the turn. Sometimes wheels locked together as chariots came too close; then there was the risk of being run down by the galloping horses behind, and that could mean injury or death.

The Roman crowd in their thousands shouted themselves hoarse as their favourites surged ahead – or lagged behind. Heavy bets were placed and money changed hands. When the race ended, the Emperor gave rich presents to the winner and the nobles, not to be outdone, added their lavish presents to the lucky charioteer. Those fearless young men could become millionaires before they were 25. But it was a dangerous game and few lived to be 30.

gladiators

GLADIATORS IN THE AMPHITHEATRE

The most famous of all the Roman public shows were also the most dreadful. Charioteers often lost their lives in the Circus, just as some modern racing-drivers are killed in races that give entertainment to thousands. But in the Roman amphitheatre, people were deliberately killed simply to give a horrible kind of excitement to the huge crowds that watched. The best known and best preserved of the amphitheatres is the Colosseum in Rome, parts of which still stand four-stories high. In the great oval arena, 206 yards (188 metres) long and 171 yards (156

Colosseum in Rome

metres) wide, 50,000 spectators watched some of the most cruel and barbaric entertainments ever staged.

The gladiators who fought in the amphitheatre were often men condemned to death for some serious crime or were prisoners taken in war. Some gladiators were professionals, just like modern professional footballers. They were trained in special schools to fight with shield and sword, dagger and small arm-shield or buckler, and with a net and three-pronged fork called a trident. There could be only one outcome to their fights – one of them had to die! When they arrived in the arena they first marched round, dressed in splendid robes embroidered in gold. Then they halted before the Emperor's royal box and cried: 'Hail, Emperor, those who are about to die salute thee!' Then the fights began, the crowds betting large sums on the outcome of each one, cheering their favourites as wounds began to tell and blood to flow. When one of the fighters was killed, his body was dragged from the arena and sand was quickly scattered to hide the blood. Then more fighters came on. And then more. Until sometimes as many as a hundred corpses had been dragged out.

Sometimes the rules were changed and no gladiator was allowed to survive the day, no matter how many fights he had won. The winner of a fight was made to fight a fresh gladiator and the winner of that fight had to fight another, until all the gladiators were dead.

To provide variety, wild animals were sometimes brought into the arena – lions, tigers, bulls, panthers, even elephants and rhinoceroses. They were made to fight each other to the death and then criminals, or those condemned for some supposed crime, were thrown to the animals that survived. For all their great civilisation and their fine buildings, the Romans could be horribly cruel. It was all ended at last by the coming of Christianity.

Now, only the great buildings of the amphitheatres remain, in ruins. Some of the relics – helmets, swords, the chains of prisoners and slaves, can be seen in museums, and pictures of fighting gladiators are a favourite subject for Roman pottery and mosaic floors.